1 MONTH OF
FREE
READ

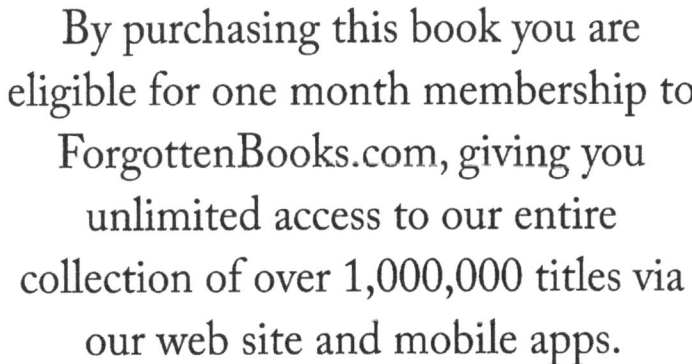

at
www.ForgottenBooks.com

By purchasing this book you are eligible for one month membership to ForgottenBooks.com, giving you unlimited access to our entire collection of over 1,000,000 titles via our web site and mobile apps.

To claim your free month visit:
www.forgottenbooks.com/free785034

English
Français
Deutsche
Italiano
Español
Português

www.forgottenbooks.com

Mythology Photography **Fiction**
Fishing Christianity **Art** Cooking
Essays Buddhism Freemasonry
Medicine **Biology** Music **Ancient
Egypt** Evolution Carpentry Physics
Dance Geology **Mathematics** Fitness
Shakespeare **Folklore** Yoga Marketing
Confidence Immortality Biographies
Poetry **Psychology** Witchcraft
Electronics Chemistry History **Law**
Accounting **Philosophy** Anthropology
Alchemy Drama Quantum Mechanics
Atheism Sexual Health **Ancient History**
Entrepreneurship Languages Sport
Paleontology Needlework Islam
Metaphysics Investment Archaeology
Parenting Statistics Criminology
Motivational

CHARGE

DELIVERED TO THE

CLERGY OF THE DIOCESE

OF

SALISBURY.

one another even as Christ hath loved and for-
given us.

So may we hope to be gradually fitted for the
reception of the Lord's choicest gift,—that our
Church may not only be pure in doctrine, and
holy in her members, but that she may also be
at unity in herself;—that " as there is but one
" Body, and one Spirit, and one hope of our
" calling, one Lord, one Faith, one Baptism, one
" God and Father of us all;—so we may hence-
" forth be all of one heart and one soul, united
" in one holy Bond of Truth and Peace, of Faith
" and Charity."

THE END.

H. W. BALL, PRINTER, WELLS.

CHARGE

ADDRESSED TO THE

CLERGY OF THE DIOCESE OF RIPON,

AT THE

TRIENNIAL VISITATION

IN SEPTEMBER, 1847.

———

BY

CHARLES-THOMAS LONGLEY, D.D.
LORD BISHOP OF RIPON.

———

LONDON:
FRANCIS & JOHN RIVINGTON,
ST. PAUL'S CHURCH YARD, AND WATERLOO PLACE.

1847.

LONDON:
GILBERT AND RIVINGTON, PRINTERS,
ST. JOHN'S SQUARE.

TO THE

CLERGY OF THE DIOCESE OF RIPON,

THIS CHARGE,

PUBLISHED AT THEIR REQUEST,

IS INSCRIBED,

WITH SINCERE AFFECTION AND RESPECT,

BY

THEIR FAITHFUL FRIEND AND BROTHER,

C. T. RIPON.

CHARGE,

&c.

My Rev. Brethren,

The lapse of ten completed years since the commencement of that spiritual relation in which we stand to each other, marks the termination of a cycle which seems more especially to invite us to such a review of the past as may serve each of us as materials of encouragement or warning for the future, in our several provinces of ministerial labour. And it is indeed well, that, amidst the ceaseless round of anxious duties in which so many of us are engaged in this populous Diocese, we should avail ourselves of every occasion that presents itself for calm meditation on our duties and responsibilities; seeking fresh supplies from the fountain of all grace to animate us in our arduous course, that so, in that great solemn day in which every man's work shall be tried, we may be able to render our account with joy. A feeling of regret may at times possibly pass over the minds of some among us, that owing to the peculiar circumstances of the Church in our day, and through the incessant demands that are made on our time and thoughts, to devise fresh expedients to meet the growing wants of our increasing flocks, we should be so much occupied in what I may call the material organization of Christ's Church, and have less time than we could wish to devote to the spiritual edification of the body of Christ; that we are compelled to a certain extent, as it were, to "leave the Word of God and serve tables," instead of "giving ourselves continually," as we could wish, "to prayer and the ministry of the Word." But, under such circumstances, while we recollect the gracious assurance, that as is our day, so shall our strength be, and that whatever burthen it may please the Lord to lay upon us, He will never allow it to render us the less competent for the work to which He has appointed us, we should the more readily profit by such seasons as the present; in the hope that a renewed blessing may descend upon us, as we retrace the course of our past ministry, and form fresh resolutions of fulfilling, through grace, our respective charges, with more of love to our flocks, and more of devotion to our blessed Master's service than ever.

The decennial period to which I have already alluded has certainly been marked by a series of greater efforts in this country for the extension of Divine truth, through the ministrations of our Church, than can be pointed to during any ten years since the Reformation. Within that date we have witnessed successive Governments, each vying with the other, according to their respective views of the exigency of the case, in devising measures to enable the Church of England more effectually to develope her energies, and adapt herself to the increasing wants of the people. Under the operation of these measures, we have seen many inveterate abuses reformed, and our revenues more beneficially applied: we have seen an increase in the Episcopate, both at home and abroad, sanctioned by the authorities of the State, and a large addition in our populous districts to the number of our Clergy labouring there. We have also seen societies either newly formed, or old ones receiving an extraordinary additional impulse to their movements; so that our Church is in every direction lengthening her cords, and strengthening her stakes. I am sure I shall be borne out in the view I have taken, when I point to the Church Endowment and Benefices Plurality Acts, and the various acts for carrying into effect the reports of the Ecclesiastical Commissioners: to the efforts of the two valuable societies which have been established for providing additional Curates and Pastoral Aid, and to the large private contributions which on several occasions have been levied, for promoting the education of the poor in the prin-- ciples of our Church, seconded as they have been by the distribution of the parliamentary grants, so large a proportion of which has been assigned to purposes connected with Church education. The fruits of all these proceedings are happily most manifest, and it may not be uninteresting or uninstructive if I set before you some statistics which will show the progress that has been made in our own Diocese, under the influence of these enconragements, between the years 1836 and 1846, in those matters which chiefly tend to the religious and moral culture of our people.

At the close of the year 1836 there were in this Diocese 295 Incumbents, 80 Curates, 300 Churches and Chapels, and 180 Glebe Houses, with 47 of the Clergy non-resident. In 1846 we find 370 Churches [1] and Chapels, and 225 Glebe Houses, 360 Incumbents, and 120 Curates, and only 27 non-resident Clergy: whence there appears an increase of seventy Churches and Chapels, besides 36 fresh Schoolrooms licensed for Divine Worship, in remote Hamlets, the latter containing accommodation for about 6000 persons: 100 additional Clergy, with 45 new Parsonage Houses built, while there has been a decrease in the number of non-resident

[1] See Appendix, Note I.

Clergy by about one-half. As regards the erection of schools, the advance has been still more striking. For although the number added during the last ten years does not exceed seventy-six [2], yet as they afford accommodation for nearly 30,000 children, it is clear that in this department we are gaining on the increase of our population; for this number will represent a population of at least 240,000, an amount far exceeding any addition which can have accrued during that period: and still, with all these efforts, the state of education in many of our parishes must continue to be a matter of great anxiety, and calls for far greater improvement both in quantity and quality.

While, however, we acknowledge the very important assistance which has been rendered to us in carrying out these various works, through the above-named channels, I should be guilty of ingratitude as well as injustice were I to refrain from alluding to two other causes which have mainly promoted these results. They are also attributable, in the first place, to that Christian liberality which has raised in this Diocese alone at the rate of £25,000 per annum, during the last eight years, towards the building and endowing churches, and the erection of parsonage houses, besides the large sums contributed for the building of schools; and secondly, to that generous devotion to the spiritual interests

---

[2] See Appendix, Note I.

of your flocks, which has prompted many of you to make sacrifices of time, and labour, and substance, in planning and promoting these works of charity, not so much in proportion to, as beyond your means and abilities. Nevertheless, the consideration of the best methods of making farther aggression on the mass of ungodliness and ignorance which still prevails in many parts of our Diocese, continues to be a subject of the gravest solicitude: and the more so, when we reflect that the funds of that chief instrument in fostering many of these objects, our Diocesan Church Building Society, are nearly exhansted. I trust, my Rev. Brethren, that both you and our brethren of the laity will co-operate with me in devising some means of speedily recruiting its finances.

But in two or three quarters, at any rate, some of you may, I hope, receive additional relief in your ministerial labours, through other measures that have been very recently adopted. The difficulties in which the Clergy of our populous districts are placed, from the inadequacy of their number to cope with the overwhelming population which surrounds them, have recently formed one of the subjects of deliberation among the Episcopal Body. The result of that discussion has been the adoption of certain [3] regulations (sanctioned by the almost unanimous approval of the Bishops), which shall

---

[3] See Appendix, Note II.

guide the employment of Scripture Readers in those Dioceses in which it may be deemed advisable to introduce them. It seems to me that every possible security has been provided which can guard the system against abuse.

The following is the general outline of the plan: Any Incumbent who proposes to employ a Scripture Reader, will name the candidate for the office to the Bishop, to be examined as regards his fitness for the office, either by the Bishop himself, or by some one appointed by him. The candidate must be a communicant in the Church of England of at least two years' standing; and if, after due inquiry and examination, he be approved, the Bishop will allow him, by a written permission, to enter on his duties as a Scripture Reader. Thus officially connected with the Church, it will be his duty to search out the ignorant and the destitute in the district, to read the Holy Scriptures from house to house, and to urge on the people the duty of availing themselves of the privileges which the Church holds out to them. He will point out to all persons the duty of attending its public services; of bringing their children to baptism, and of sending them afterwards to school, while he directs the parents and the people generally to seek farther instruction and edification from their spiritual pastors.

The Scripture Readers will thus form a connecting link between the Parochial Clergy and those of their parishioners who from various circumstances are beyond the reach of their own pastoral superintendence. They will be directed to carry with them in their visits no book but the Holy Scriptures and the Prayer-Book, and such volumes as may be sanctioned by the Incumbent, and they will be strictly forbidden to preach in houses or elsewhere.

To the operation of such a system as this in our populous districts, if it be carried out in the spirit in which it has been framed, I cannot but look forward with feelings of much hopefulness. It must be known to many whom I now address, that there are to be found, from time to time, young men of the middle classes, piously disposed and spiritually minded characters, who would willingly do the work of an Evangelist, and are capable of it, in its humbler departments ; but finding no sphere for the exercise of this their talent within the pale of the Church, they are continually tempted to seek it within the ranks of dissent, and not unfrequently yield to the temptation. If this plan be adopted in my own Diocese, and the result, as I fully anticipate, be successful, I should not feel disinclined, considering the very inadequate supply of Curates, to admit as candidates for Deacon's orders, those persons who shall have undergone satisfactorily a two years' probation as Scripture Readers in this Diocese, although they may not have passed through any course of Collegiate education, in case they shall be specially recommended to me by the Incumbent who has employed them, and always provided they prove equal to the examination to which candidates for that order are at present submitted.

Whilst, therefore, I trust that this measure will afford some relief to many of my Reverend Brethren whose labours are at present beyond their strength, I look forward with still greater satisfaction to the effects of those measures which have been adopted by the Committee of Privy Council on Education, with such general consent on the part of the Legislature. I am persuaded that I can have no more faithful and competent witnesses than yourselves to the fact, that the system which existed previously to their adoption was still inadequate to meet the emergency, in spite of the repeated efforts that were made to stimulate public liberality. I am too well conversant with the struggles and difficulties with which so many of you have had to contend, first of all in erecting your schools, and afterwards in your persevering efforts to raise the contributions necessary for their maintenance, not to claim confidently your testimony to the necessity of some more effectual and permanent support to your exertions than they had ever yet received; for although your difficulties in erecting schools were, as we have seen, not insurmountable, there still remained the constant bur-

then of annually raising the amount of the teachers'
salaries, and the sum necessary for the current
expenses of the school, which in some instances
pressed so heavily as to lead to the ultimate closing
of the school. And while this can be with truth
asserted of the statistics of education within the
Church, that necessity has been irrefragably proved
to be still more urgent beyond its limits. Nor
ought the Government of this country to have
refrained from lending more ample assistance, if
ever it hoped to see our vast population trained up
in the fear of God, in the faith of Christ, and with
a proper knowledge of their duties as Christian
citizens. If, indeed, every member of the community so felt the obligations which his station, his
wealth, or his competence imposed upon him, as
that each would spontaneously contribute his due
proportion for the public service of his country,
then would legislative interference be superfluous
in our national finances, and voluntary taxation
in every department would supersede all legal
exaction. But what would be the resources of our
public Exchequer were such the only mode of
providing for the defence of the country through
its fleets and armies, for the administration of jus-
tice, and for the various contingencies of our civil
expenditure? And what reason have we to sup-
pose, that, amidst so much infirmity of principle
and purpose as unhappily prevails, it would fare

better with the general education of the people, if it be left entirely to the voluntary system? The result that might have been reasonably anticipated, has been abundantly realized; and the condition of many parts of our manufacturing parishes, as well as of some, I fear, of our agricultural districts, together with the disheartening records of our prisons and penitentiaries, in spite of all that has been done so wisely and so zealously, conclusively proves the failure of this mode of accomplishing the complete education of the lower orders in this country. "The impotence of the voluntary principle," then, as that lamented Christian philanthropist, Dr. Chalmers, in his almost dying words proclaimed, "has now been fully established." The system has been fairly on its trial for nearly half a century. Various convulsive efforts have been made from time to time to inspire it with a vigour commensurate to the emergency; but they only served to lead the mind of the Legislature, and of the vast bulk of intelligence in the country, to the irresistible conclusion, that more extensive aid on the part of the Government was indispensable, if any effectual remedy were to be applied to the mass of moral evil which prevailed. It is needless to recapitulate the several attempts which have been made by successive Governments to supply the want so generally acknowledged and so deeply felt by the Clergy themselves. The result of all these efforts seems to me to prove that any scheme that should ultimately secure a permanent sanction, must be such as would not supplant those institutions which were already engaged in the work of educating the lower orders, but support and enable them more effectually to fulfil the purposes for which they were established.

By those, therefore, who entertained these views, the Plan of the Government, as developed in the Minutes of Council on Education of August and December, 1846, could not but be regarded with sincere approval. Those Minutes do not, indeed, profess to accomplish that which many persons, nevertheless, hold to be incumbent on every Government, where the difficulties are not insuperable, as in this country, at the present moment, they must be confessed to be. They do not propound a grand and comprehensive scheme of national education which shall relieve the Church and Dissenters alike from all responsibility in providing for the better education of those children of the poorer classes that belong to them respectively; but they rather increase their responsibilities, by holding out greater encouragements than were ever before offered, for vigorously prosecuting their endeavours to train them up in the knowledge of God's Holy Word, and obedience to its precepts.

And among the many evidences of practical wisdom which seem to be exhibited in the course recently pursued in this matter by the Government, I would remark, that while its ultimate purpose is to promote the general education of the people, it has in the first instance directed its chief endeavours rather towards improving the quality of the instruction already imparted than increasing the material part by the erection of additional schools. The public mind has become more and more strongly impressed with the conviction that there is little hope of raising the standard of Christian education, unless a class of teachers can be produced whose high moral and religious tone shall penetrate the whole course of instruction given, and animate throughout the system which they direct; unless there be that in the mutual intercourse subsisting between master and scholar, which shall insensibly kindle in the breast of the pupils a desire to imitate the preceptor's example, and to frame their own character after the model thus exhibited to them: a teaching which shall imbue the children with sound principles not only by precept and positive instruction, but also and chiefly through the imperceptible influence of that Christian bearing which is witnessed in the words and actions, in the whole course and tenor of the master's life. It is to further, in various ways, this deeply important object, that the Minutes of Council above referred to are almost exclusively framed. With an ultimate view to this end it is, that inducements are held out to the most promising children at our National Schools, to remain there as paid monitors or pupil teachers, with the further hope that when they are of sufficient age to enter a training school, they may receive the aid of the State in preparing themselves for the office of schoolmaster : that when installed in that office, a competent salary will be provided for them through the help of the State : that they may, if found duly qualified by a Government Inspector, receive assistance in the conduct of their Schools, through paid monitors or pupil teachers : and that when age and infirmity shall have deprived them of the power of thus gaining their subsistence, they may have earned a pension for their support in their declining years. In all these provisions we witness a wise and salutary recognition, on the part of the State, of the value it attaches to this too long neglected class of public servants.

The condition on which this seasonable assistance is offered to our schools, is that they be open to the visits of a Government Inspector. I believe that much of the apprehension which for a while prevailed in the minds of many of the Clergy on this subject has disappeared; and that there is now so general an impression as to the beneficial effect of inspection, and so general a willingness to admit it, that these functionaries are universally welcomed as important auxiliaries in the field of instruction. In the first instance, the offer of salaries to masters conducting schools was confined to such as had been trained for one, two, or three years, at a Normal school: but that privilege is now extended to any teachers of schools complying with the above condition, and who shall prove themselves, after examination, worthy to receive the boon: and it will be for each of you, my Rev. Brethren, to exert yourselves in your respective spheres, to raise the standard of your schools to that level, in point of knowledge and discipline, which shall qualify them to become partakers in these benefits. In cases where your schools are already in a promising state as to attainment and organization, you will at once apply to the Committee of Privy Council, soliciting them to take the necessary measures for certifying the fitness of your master to receive the Government grant of one-third of his salary, if the other two-thirds are raised by private contributions, and likewise the fitness of one or more of your most proficient scholars, to be selected as apprentices to the master or mistress. And herein do we perceive a great collateral advantage in the system, that it will give so great a stimulus to exertion in schools already founded; not only because the masters will strive to place themselves within reach of the benefit thus held out to them, but also because the necessary condition of inspection will tend to infuse fresh life and vigour into their operations.

By many of you, my Rev. Brethren, it will, I

B 2

am sure, be felt to be a most happy coincidence, that these movements on the part of the Government should have been contemporaneous with the enactment of that bill which limits the hours of labour in the factories: a measure which promises so much for the moral and social improvement of the lower classes in our manufacturing districts.

Upon a review of the whole bearing of these Minutes, one cannot but conclude that, of all the schemes which have ever yet been proposed by the State for the acceptance of the Church, this is the one which most commends itself to the unanimous approval of her members. It leaves the operations of the Clergymen and of the School Committee entirely unfettered in the management of the school, and merely enables them more effectually to develope the system they were already pursuing, by securing a larger stipend for the master, and for the scholars the benefit of an increase of teachers. Nor can we fail to rejoice in seeing these amicable relations thus established in this matter between the Church and the State. I abstain at present from discussing the Minute of Council that has subsequently appeared, which seems to intimate a willingness on the part of the Committee to make grants for secular education alone, without reference to religion. I trust that this unpromising appearance may admit of satisfactory explanation.

If, my Rev. Brethren, I have dwelt longer on

the topic of education than you might have expected, you will, I hope, attribute it to my conviction, that until the Christian training and instruction of our youth is carried forward on a scale of greater improvement, as well as greater extension, than heretofore, the Church can never effectually fulfil her duties towards them in their riper years, nor will the prosperity of our country ever be based on a really solid foundation.

As another topic of encouragement under the pressure of your ministerial labours, I would point to that recent decision of the Court of Queen's Bench, which pronounces certain attempts that have of late years been made to evade the law of church-rates to be illegal. In no part of England have those obstructions contributed more to increase the embarrassments of the Clergy, than in this Diocese; and I trust that many of you, my Rev. Brethren, will derive substantial relief from this important enunciation of the law. It is therein recognized to be imperative upon the parishioners to repair the fabric of the Church; and although occasional difficulties may still possibly arise, a great point has been gained in having this principle laid down upon such high authority. For we may believe that many who resisted the proposal of a church-rate while they imagined this point to be doubtful, will shrink as much, for conscience sake, from evading the law, as they would from openly violating it.

They will now have learnt that it is in vain to propose any general amendment, either postponing the subject for an indefinite period, or refusing the rate as unscriptural; for this is tantamount to an assertion on the part of the parish vestry that they have a right to dispense with the laws of England; and they will find, that by supporting such amendment, they render their votes as invalid as if they were absent from the meeting. It is upon this principle that the minority may in law be considered an unanimous majority in favour of the rate proposed; that being the only legal question before the meeting, and every legal vote being for that. The numerical majority, on the other hand, are held to be silent; and by their silence to have assented to the legal acts of the minority; they are held to have thrown away their votes, because they used their votes in attempting to defeat the law, instead of carrying it into effect. As to the course which each of you, my Rev. Brethren, should pursue, in case your church-rate be factiously objected to, when it is admittedly necessary, it would seem advisable, that after the motion for the rate has been made, the chairman should repeatedly inquire whether any parishioner has any other proposal to make. If any amendment shall be offered which does not go to ascertaining the amount of rate to be levied, or the mode of levying it, it is the duty of the chairman to decline putting it to the meeting as irrelevant: should no other proposal be made, let the chairman at once put the motion to the meeting, and at the same time warn those present, that as there is one proposition only before them, and that, for the purpose of discharging the obligation imposed upon them by law, all persons present who abstain from voting for it, will be considered as assenting to it, on the principle above referred to.

Proceeding beyond the limits of our own Diocese, we cannot but acknowledge it to be a subject of mutual congratulation, that the Legislature has at length publicly sanctioned the principle, that some addition to the number of Bishops in England and Wales is necessary for the efficient government and oversight of our Church. The only marvel is, that this recognition should have been so tardy; and that in these days, the only expedient for providing more effectual episcopal superintendence of the more populous districts, should at first have been found in the union of ancient sees. It was throughout my own deliberate conviction, that in the case of the Dioceses of St. Asaph and Bangor, that union never would take place: that the growing desire for an increased Episcopacy was running counter to the spirit of an arrangement which seemed to regard such extension as hopeless, and merely cast about for the best means of adjusting more equitably the very disproportionate labours of the respective Diocesans, without altering their existing number. The reports, however, of the first Ecclesiastical Commission, and the subsequent enactments based upon them, so far from leading the minds of Churchmen to acquiesce in the conclusion that any farther enlargement was impracticable, served but to invite reflection to the subject. The retrospect of the past, and the fact that although the population had nearly quadrupled since the Reformation, not one Bishop had been added to the number of the Church's spiritual rulers since the reign of Henry VIII., has led, as might most reasonably be expected, to the almost unanimous conviction that a farther division of our Sees, and a still farther multiplication of the number of those who are to take the oversight of the Church, is necessary for its efficient government. Now history tells us that Henry VIII. had matured a plan for increasing the number of Bishops to sixty-six, and it was to have been carried into execution by the endowment of twenty additional Sees, as well as the appointment of twenty-six Suffragan Bishops. Of the additional Sees, five only were created. The act which provided for the creation of Suffragans, was passed in the year 1534. It continues to this day in our Statute Book, and in it are enumerated the twenty-six localities [1]

[1] These were, Thetford, Ipswich, Colchester, Dover, Guildford, Southampton, Taunton, Shaftesbury, Molton, Marlborough,

which were to become their seats; but so much has the relative population of different places changed, that Hull is the only town in Yorkshire included in the list, while in Lancashire there is not one named. For all practical purposes, therefore, that act is, at the present moment, little more than a dead letter, save in so far as it strengthens the argument, à fortiori, for the increase of the Episcopate in these our days, when our population is multiplying to so overwhelming an amount [2].

But it is often urged, in answer to this plea for increasing the number of the chief or subordinate Pastors of our Church, that it is invalid, seeing that the various Dissenting bodies bear so large a proportion to the whole. But you will yourselves be fully conscious, my Reverend Brethren, that the labours of the Clergy are not limited to those alone who are regularly in communion with our Church; and that a large share of your time and toil is often bestowed on persons who are more or less connected with other religious communities. As an

Bedford, Leicester, Gloucester, Shrewsbury, Bristol, Penrith, Bridgewater, Nottingham, Grantham, Hull, Huntingdon, Cambridge, Pereth, Berwick, St. German's (Cornwall), the Isle of Wight.—See Burnet's Hist. of Reformation, book ii.

[2] The population of the territory afterwards included within the Diocese of Ripon, increased between the years 1831 and 1841, from 760,000 to 916,000; and there can be no doubt that it now exceeds 1,000,000.

answer to this current objection, it may be interesting to you to gather from the abstract of the registration returns some approximation to the ratio which the members of the Church of England bear to the rest of the people. The calculation refers to England and Wales alone; and it appears that in a given year, since the Registration Act was passed, of the marriages performed, ninety per cent. were solemnized in the Church of England; of those who were interred, eighty-five per cent. were buried according to her rites, and by her Ministers, and of those baptized, seventy per cent. were admitted into the Church according to the form prescribed by our Liturgy. That many of those who thus partake of the rites of our Church are merely nominal members of it, must with pain be admitted; but it is equally clear that they cannot be claimed by any other religious body; and that the proportion above named is actually demanding the labour of our Clergy in the administration of her offices. These, then, are the materials on which the fostering care and spiritual energies of the Church must be brought to bear, in the hopes of leading them into faithful and active communion with her, so that they may bring forth the fruits worthy of their high calling in Christ Jesus: these are the masses for whom our Clergy are daily engaged in providing, as well in matters which concern their temporal as their spiritual wants.

If we look, then, merely to the vast addition which is year by year made to the numbers of our people, we should infer the necessity of a corresponding increase not only of the Parochial Clergy, but also of those whose province it is to take the oversight of the Church. This, however, would give but an imperfect view of the bearings of the case, as regards the Episcopate; for the labours of that body may be said to increase, as it were, in a geometrical proportion. The increased zeal and activity of the Parochial Clergy, which I cannot but acknowledge with feelings of thankfulness and admiration, throw an additional burthen on their Diocesans, which they rejoice indeed to bear, so long as health and strength are granted them to support it. No one can be acquainted with the internal operations of a Diocese without perceiving that the existence of those numerous societies which have been founded within the last few years to aid the Church in carrying out her spiritual ministrations, whether belonging to one Diocese alone, or embracing all equally, while they frequently demand the Bishop's counsel and superintendence, furnish occasion for an indefinite increase of correspondence with his Clergy on the various subjects connected with them.

If, indeed, the Church expects her Bishops to act merely as the censors and correctors of their Clergy, and to discharge a certain round of prescribed official duties, which may be measured by the public eye, and are patent to universal observation, it might perhaps be questioned whether their numbers were not commensurate with their functions; and yet in the matter of Confirmations alone, it were much to be desired (according to my own impression at least), that they could be more frequent, and that the numbers assembled, which have been already lessened by the division of districts, might be still more reduced by farther subdivision, were not this incompatible with the pressure of our other obligations. But if the Episcopate is to be regarded, by our people generally, not merely as a name, but as a living reality, a vital energizing principle; if our Bishops are to identify themselves with their Clergy and their people, to throw their hearts and minds into their Dioceses, to be known among their flocks as St. Paul was among his; to be the friends, the fathers, and the counsellors of their Clergy, advising them in their difficulties, arbitrating in differences, peace-makers where their influence can avail, resolving cases of conscience where propounded, forwarding by their counsel every good work and labour of love; if they are to be able to judge with their own eyes as to the practical working of each Clergyman in his parish, to strengthen their hands in their hours of trial and perplexity, to encourage the timid and arouse the lukewarm, to let each congregation hear from time to time, from their own lips, the words of eternal truth, and the poor parents of every parish see that besides their own appointed minister, there is the chief pastor of the Diocese who cares for the souls of their children, and is furthering plans for their spiritual benefit: if, I say, these weighty charges really press upon a Bishop, I know not who can be sufficient for these things, according to the present constitution of our Dioceses. To say that I am myself unequal to so great a burthen, would avail but little in the argument, for I can well anticipate the ready reply; but I do conscientiously believe that the exertion of body and mind, which a full response to all those demands in addition to his ordinary official duties must require, would be far beyond the usual average of physical strength and mental ability.

Nor is the picture which I have here attempted to draw the creature merely of my own imagination. Such is the portrait presented to us by historians and biographers of those great and good men who, in times when the constitution of our Dioceses admitted of such an administration of them, have best adorned their high office by the holiness of their lives, and the abundance of their labours, and whose praise is in all the churches. Such is the view taken of a Bishop's duties by the framers of our Services, and such are the obligations imposed upon us by our vows of Consecration. Therein we promised to instruct the people committed to our charge out of the Holy Scriptures, teaching and exhorting with wholesome doctrine; as well as to maintain, and set forward, as much as shall lie in us, quietness, love, and peace, not merely among our Clergy, but among all men. Therein prayer was offered for us, that we might be evermore ready to spread abroad the Gospel of our Lord Jesus Christ, the glad tidings of reconciliation with God. Therein were we charged, to hold up the weak, to heal the sick, to bind up the broken; to bring again the outcasts, and to seek the lost. Therein were we warned, by the injunction of St. Paul, that we should be "apt to teach," and by his example that we should "feed the Church of God which He hath purchased with His blood." We were reminded how St. Paul taught publicly, and from house to house, and ceased not to warn every one night and day, with tears, and how he was willing to part with life itself, if he could but finish with joy that ministry which he had received of the Lord Jesus, the ministry of the Gospel of the grace of God.

But passing from the Service of Consecration itself, we cannot glance at the Epistles of St. Paul without observing how fully these lineaments are filled up, in all their practical detail, in the course of his general oversight over the whole of his flock.

From them we learn his deep sympathy with his people in all their trials either from within or from without. "Who is weak," says he, "and I am not weak? who is offended, and I burn not?" He tells them that though absent from them in the body, he was present in spirit, being comforted in their comfort; his joy being the joy of them all; how his people were in his heart, to live and die with them; to spend and be spent for them: how he exhorted and comforted them as a father doth his children; was gentle among them, even as a nurse cherisheth her children; being affectionately desirous of them, and willing to impart to them, not the Gospel of God only, but his own soul also, because they were so dear to him.

And while the records of Holy Scripture, the language of the Church, as well as the lives of those who have shone forth as the brightest patterns to such as should come after them, all witness to the same truth as to our duties and our office, I must be permitted to add yet one more testimony. You are yourselves, my Rev. Brethren, in some measure responsible for what I have written: for you have yourselves taught me, during the ten years' intercourse I have had the happiness of holding with you, that such is the estimate you entertain of what a Bishop's functions should be; and such the relation in which, were it in these days possible, you would fain have your Diocesan stand towards you. This relation I feel it indeed a privilege to hold, while the one painful reflection which accompanies it, is the utter impossibility, arranged as our Dioceses now are, of realizing all that is involved in it, coupled with the recollection of the very imperfect manner in which its obligations have already been discharged, as well as the anticipation that they must be yet more imperfectly fulfilled, when increasing years and declining strength shall have further impaired the ability to perform them. I acknowledge, however, with thankfulness, that the assistance which many of you, my Rev. Brethren, have kindly and considerately promised to render me by undertaking the office of Rural Dean ³, will tend in some degree to lighten the labours of your Bishop, and to render the administration of affairs more efficient, as I hope, throughout the Diocese.

The time seems then to have arrived, my Rev. Brethren, when the Church of England will be called upon to decide whether she be content to acquiesce in the position, that she shall have overseers who can take no such effectual oversight of the flock as her services contemplate: that the evils which have resulted from this state of things shall not only continue without a remedy, but shall be indefinitely aggravated, as the population of the country increases; and this without any

³ See Appendix, Note III.

hope of mitigation. Surely, my ·Rev. Brethren, that such a condition of things should be perpetuated, is morally impossible. It never can be, that while every other religious community in this country has full liberty to multiply the number of its superior functionaries, according to the requirements of the times, as the general body increases, and the subordinate ministers are consequently multiplied, the Church of England shall be the only one proscribed from ever adding to the amount of her spiritual rulers; alone denied the power of adapting herself to existing exigencies, and of giving free scope to all her various energies. The principle of periodical increase has happily been recognized in the gradual development of our Church in the Colonies; and I never can believe but that it will likewise, from time to time, be acted upon in the economy of the Church at home.

Before I conclude my remarks upon the general condition of the Church, you will not, I am sure, expect me to refrain from touching upon the aspect of that movement which has agitated the Church during the last fifteen years, and in which so remarkable a change has taken place since we last met on an occasion like this; and I shall touch upon it but briefly, because of the opportunities afforded me since my last Visitation [4], of expressing generally my sentiments thereupon. And, in turn-

---

[4] See Appendix, Note IV.

ing our thoughts towards those who have recently
quitted the communion of our Church for that of
Rome, painful as the retrospect may in some re-
spects be, it is so far consoling to reflect that not
one licensed Clergyman in this Diocese has thus
renounced his vows of ordination; that among the
Laity belonging to the Church within it, the instances have been so very rare of persons abjuring
its principles for those of Rome. As to those mis-
guided persons who have fallen into this grievous
error, in passing our judgment upon them, we may
well adopt the mild spirit of that eloquent passage
of Bishop Jeremy Taylor [5], wherein he says, " I see
it is possible for a man to believe any thing he
hath a mind to; and this seems to me to have been
permitted to reprove the vanity of man's imagination, and the confidence of opinion, and make us
humble, apt to learn, inquisitive, charitable ;" adding
afterwards, " It will concern the wisest man alive
to be diligent in his search, modest in his sentences,
to prejudge no man ; to reprove his adversaries
with meekness, and a spirit conscious of human
weakness, and aptness to be abused." It will then, I
think, be most becoming in us to view with a spirit
of deep compassion, the fall of those who have
abandoned the communion of that Church which
was their own first spiritual home, as well as that

---

[5] Epistle Dedicatory to the Treatise on the Real Presence.

of their fathers before them. To forsake houses, and lands, and country, brethren and sisters, father and mother, for Christ's sake and the Gospel's, is indeed a sacrifice worthy of a Christian's self-devotion : but to see well-meaning, but deluded, persons renounce all these, and embrace poverty, with the loss of friends and kindred too, in order to vow allegiance to a Church which not only persists, in spite of centuries of remonstrance, in countenancing idolatry, but has usurped the place of Christ, disparaging His authority, by refusing communion with the Church of God, upon the conditions on which Christ Himself instructed His Apostles to receive disciples, and by forbidding believers to partake of the Lord's Supper after the manner of our Saviour's original institution;—here is indeed a spectacle which may well awaken feelings of the truest pity; feelings which will not be mitigated by the anticipation of that disappointment that awaits many of them, when a deeper insight into the system they have embraced shall have revealed the whole truth to them : nor by the testimony which some of them have unhappily given, of the baneful influence on their Christian temper that has passed over them since they adopted their new profession. I am well aware that indiscriminate invective will surely recoil upon the head of him who uses it, and will rather disparage than strengthen the soundest cause. But there is a tone and a language which truth imperatively demands when we are dealing with the dangerous errors of the Church of Rome: and one cannot but lament that so many in the present day are to be found who, instead of using the language of those stern, masculine, and uncompromising protests that abound in the works not only of our Reformers themselves, but also of so many learned Fathers of the English Church subsequent to the age of the Reformation, such as Jewell, Hall, Taylor, and Barrow, Bramhall, and Usher, and Bull, are prone to adopt a spurious liberality, a latitudinarian indifference, under the cloak of charity, which confounds right and wrong, truth and error, and seems to represent it to be matter of as little moment whether we abide in the Church of our baptism and ordination, or abandon it for the Church of Rome, as whether we quit or remain in a given Diocese. I trust, however, that much has been done to check those secessions; and that recent events in this Diocese, as elsewhere, will prove how dangerous it is to try how near we can approach forbidden ground without actually transgressing the limits proposed by the Church of England, and how necessary it is to confine ourselves to that line of teaching which she has clearly and expressly pointed out to us. I would hope, too, that one event, in particular, which occurred last year, will impress upon you, my Reverend Brethren, the importance of complying with an injunction which I addressed to you in a former Charge; and that you will never, on any account, introduce a Clergyman to officiate regularly in your parishes, without first offering me the opportunity of inquiry as to his character and principles.

It will then be our parts to gather its appropriate instruction from all that has occurred, and to endeavour to impress on the younger members of our Church, and more especially upon our younger Clergy, the lessons of warning and of wisdom which they teach.

In the first place, let us observe the baneful effect of that idolatry of man which induces weak minds to surrender all those ordinary means of forming a sound judgment which are in mercy abundantly vouchsafed to us, and to yield a blind deference to the dicta of some favoured leader, who happens to be distinguished for piety and learning. Such persons do not seem to be aware, that while they are habitually denouncing the principle of private judgment, they are, in fact, acting upon it, to the practical subversion of legitimate authority; for they prefer yielding an implicit obedience to the private judgment of one individual, to accepting the deliberate, public, recognized judgment of their own Church. Nor do they seem to be aware of another inconsistency, into which those who have this Romanizing tendency are apt to fall; that while it is their avowed principle to inculcate a deeper reverence for things sacred, that most sacred of all things, the Word of God itself, is usually treated with the greatest disrespect and irreverence. Of this we have a very striking illustration in the celebrated " Essay on Development." The author professes to investigate Christianity from the records of history, and we should, in the first instance, naturally look for such traces of its character as are to be found either formally or incidentally recorded in the Word of God: but this portion of history, the only inspired portion, the only portion which contains truth without any admixture of error, is studiously and disrespectfully passed by. It is difficult to over-rate the importance to the cause of truth, of the appearance of such a volume at such a period. If, indeed, the Church of Rome requires the avowal of such principles to uphold its pretensions; if the most recent advocate of her system is compelled, in so doing, to acknowledge that there is no such thing as abstract divine truth, but that the developing power of the Church may stamp that tenet with falsehood which it held for truth before, without any charge of inconsistency, then, indeed, may we see how rotten must be the foundation which needs such desperate resources to prop it up; and if I did not most truly believe that there was much more risk, from the perusal of that volume, of a young man becoming a confirmed sceptic than a Romanist, I would almost recommend it as the best antidote against a Romanizing tendency.

The volume must, at any rate, prove a valuable warning to many, revealing, as it does, and, happily, with a startling abruptness, the danger into which those who follow its author will be led, of renouncing entirely all reliance on the written Word of God; and it will be well that our Clergy should fortify themselves with those unanswerable arguments against the pretensions and corrupt practices of the Church of Rome which are set forth in the works of those powerful defenders of the Protestant doctrine whom I have before mentioned.

But amidst all the turmoils of the world, and the divisions of the Church, may we, my Reverend Brethren, find our comfort in meekly and zealously fulfilling those sacred duties which it has pleased God to lay upon us, and in living to Him who died for us. Let the weight of our responsibilities be felt more than the weight of our dignity, remembering that the Pastor's real power consists, not in the high assumption of authority, but in the influence which the spirit of love will always gain over the hearts of men; that our province is to lead men in the ways of everlasting life, rather than to force them to courses for which they are not yet prepared; and that, if we forget the example of our blessed Lord, who ever dealt so tenderly with the previous habits and preconceived opinions of those who followed Him, we are impairing the efficacy of our own ministry, and weakening the influence of the whole body of the Church. Let us rather give full proof of our ministry in the way that St. Paul exhibited his, by being "in labours more abundant," and being equally zealous of the honour of our Heavenly Master, that in nothing we disparage the cause of His Holy Gospel by carelessness, or slothfulness, or worldliness, which will surely lead to a yet more grievous fall.

And, withal, let us follow peace with all men; and if controversy there needs must be, let it chiefly consist in a Christian rivalry, as to which shall bear the deepest impress of his Heavenly Master's spirit; which shall be the most loving, and gentle, and easy to be intreated; which the most earnest in his efforts, and the most fervent in his prayers, for the souls which are committed to his keeping; which shall win most sinners to his Saviour's service; which shall wear the brightest crown, when He comes, who hath declared, "Behold, I come quickly, and my reward is with me, to give every man according as his work shall be."

APPENDIX.

Note I.

Parish.	Church.
Aldborough . . .	Roecliffe.
Almondbury . . .	Meltham Mills, Milnesbridge.
Birstall	Robertown.
Bradford	Denholme.
Garforth, church rebuilt and enlarged.	
Gargrave	Cold Coniston.
Guiseley	Yeadon.
Halifax	Queen's Head.
Keighley	Oakworth.
Kildwick	Cowling.
Kirby Malzard . . .	Grewelthorpe.
Leeds	St. Andrew's, St. Saviour's.
Mirfield	Hopton.
Ripon	Markington.
Rothwell	Middleton.
South Stainley, church rebuilt, with increased accommodation.	

Parish.	Church.
Thornhill	Whitley.
Wakefield	St. Andrew's.
Whitkirk	Seacroft.

SCHOOLS BUILT IN THE DIOCESE OF RIPON IN THE
YEARS 1844, 1845, 1846.

1844.

	Accommodation for Scholars.
Cononley	146
Battyeford	524
Horbury	350
Meltham	180
Addingham	250
Honley	523
Almondbury	300
Croft	132
Cross-stone	250
Coley	300
New Leeds (Bradford)	357
Cowgill	80
Yeadon	250
Earl's Heaton	300
Lindley	270
Stanningley	250
Leeds (St. Peter's)	685
Ditto (St. Andrew's)	504
Kirkstall	500
Leeds (St. James's)	515
Skipton (Christ Church) . . .	148
Wrenthorpe	200
Manningham	300
	7314

1845.

Accommodation
for Scholars.

Dent	200
Lofthouse	200
Pudsey, Far Town	200
Wakefield, East Moor	320
Otley	300
Wetherby	346
Headingley	200
Kirkheaton	300
Leeming	210
Elland	530
Grassington	130
Dalton	90
Lower Houses	100
Bedale	250
East Ardsley	200
Scammonden	82
	3658

1846.

Wakefield (Trinity church) . . .	300
Huddersfield (St. Paul's) . . .	596
Thurgoland	200
Birstall	339
Bramley (Whichcote)	170
Leeds (Burley)	200
Embsay	144
Farnley	335
Leeds (St. Mary)	100
Ditto (New Town)	510
Halifax (Queen's Head) . . .	400

44

	Accommodation for Scholars.
Oxenhope	208
Batley Carr	414
Idle	300
Eccup in Addle	76
	4292

Note II.

THE FOLLOWING DECLARATION WAS AGREED TO AT A MEETING OF THE BISHOPS, HELD ON THE FIRST OF JULY, 1847.

We, the undersigned, are of opinion, that whenever the Bishop of any Diocese shall sanction the employment of Scripture Readers by his Clergy, the following Rules are proper to be observed.

W. Cantuar.	C. T. Ripon.
E. Ebor.	E. Sarum.
C. J. London.	E. Norwich.
E. Dunelm.	T. Hereford.
C. R. Winton.	G. Peterborough.
J. Lincoln.	H. Worcester.
C. Bangor.	C. St. David's.
G. Rochester.	T. St. Asaph.
E. Llandaff.	A. T. Chichester.
J. B. Chester.	J. Lichfield.
R. Bath and Wells.	T. Ely.
J. H. Gloucester and Bristol.	S. Oxon.

Proposed Regulations for the Employment of Scripture Readers.

1. The object of appointing Scripture Readers being to give to the Clergy increased means of parochial efficiency, it will be the duty of the Scripture Reader, acting under the direction of the Clergyman, to search out the most destitute and ignorant of the parishioners; to read the holy Scriptures from house to house; and to urge upon the people the duty of availing themselves of all the privileges afforded them by the Church.

2. The Scripture Reader shall in every case be nominated by the Minister of the parish to the Bishop, to be examined, as to his fitness for the office, either by the Bishop himself, or by persons appointed by him for that purpose.

3. On approval, he shall be permitted by the Bishop, in writing under his hand, to enter upon his duties as Scripture Reader.

4. No person shall be appointed to the office of Scripture Reader, who has not been a communicant in the Church of England for at least two years past.

5. The Scripture Reader shall be under the control and direction of the Clergyman by whom he is nominated; who may suspend him from the exercise of his functions, giving one month's notice thereof to the Bishop; and also, except in case of misconduct, to the Reader himself.

6. No Scripture Reader shall be continued in any parish, or district, against the will of the officiating minister.

7. The Scripture Reader shall be strictly prohibited from carrying about with him, for the purpose of reading

to the people, or of distributing among them, any book, or publication, but the Scriptures of the Old and New Testament, and the Book of Common Prayer, and such other books as shall be sanctioned in writing by the Incumbent; taking care to avoid, as much as possible, all controversy.

8. The Scripture Reader shall be strictly forbidden to preach, either in houses or elsewhere.

9. He is to urge upon all persons the duty of attending the public worship of God in the Church; to inculcate upon parents the duty of bringing their children to Baptism, of training them up in the way in which they should go, and of procuring for them instruction in the parochial week-day and Sunday schools: and he is to direct them to seek for further edification and comfort in the ministrations of their appointed pastors.

10. The Scripture Reader shall keep a regular journal of each day's proceedings, noting carefully the parties visited, and the portions of Scripture read to them on each occasion; such journal to be submitted to the Clergyman at such times as he shall direct, and to be deposited with him at the end of every three months.

11. The names of all Scripture Readers, thus permitted by the Bishop in any Diocese, shall be entered in a register, to be kept in such manner as the Bishop shall direct.

Note III.

LIST OF RURAL DEANS.

ARCHDEACONRY OF RICHMOND.

DEANERY OF CATTERICK.—*Eastern Division.*

Catterick.	Kirklington.
Tunstall.	Pickhill.
Hipswell.	Leeming.
Hudswell.	Kirby Fleetham.
Hornby.	Well.
Patrick Brompton.	Wath.
Hunton.	Tanfield.
Thornton Watlass.	Bolton on Swale.
Bedale.	Burneston.
Crakehall.	Scruton.

Rural Dean, The Rev. H. P. HAMILTON, *Rector of Wath.*

Western Division.

Horsehouse.	East Witton.
Lunds.	Hawkeswell.
Hardrow.	Coverham.
Hawes.	Wensley.
Askrigg.	Leyburn.
Aysgarth.	Fingall.
Bolton.	Thornton Steward.
Redmire.	Spennithorn.
Stallingbusk.	Bellerby.
West Witton.	

Rural Dean, Rev. EDWD. WYVILL, *Rector of Fingall.*

DEANERY OF RICHMOND.—*Western Division.*

Richmond.	Grinton.
Trinity Church.	Melbecks.
Romaldkirk.	Marrick.
Laithkirk.	Downholme.
Startforth.	Marske.
Rokeby.	Barningham.
Wycliffe.	Kirby Ravensworth.
Brignall.	Dalton.
Hutton.	Forcett.
Gilling.	Easby.
Arkengarthdale.	Brompton on Swale.
Muker.	Bowes.

Rural Dean, Rev. SCOTT FRED. SURTEES, *Rector of Richmond, Yorkshire.*

Eastern Division.

Manfield.	Yafforth.
Cleasby.	Ainderby Steeple.
Barton.	Langton on Swale.
Middleton Tyas.	Kirby Wisk.
Croft.	Melsonby.
Eryholme.	Cowton South.
Great Smeaton.	Stanwick.
Cowton East.	Caldwell.
Danby Wisk.	

Rural Dean, Rev. CHAS. DODGSON, *Rector of Croft.*

DEANERY OF BOROUGHBRIDGE.—*Northern Division.*

Cundall.	Kirby Hill.
Norton le Clay.	Aldbro'.

Borobridge.   Staveley.
Lower Dunsforth.   Great Ouseburn.
Marton and Grafton.   Little Ouseburn.
Copgrove.   Nun Monkton.
Burton Leonard.   Roecliffe.

Rural Dean, Rev. JOHN CHARGE, *Rector of Copgrove.*

Southern Division.

Knaresborough.   Nidd.
Farnham.   Allerton Mauleverer.
Arkendale.   Whixley.
Brearton.   South Stainley.
Hunsingore.   High Harrogate.
Goldsborough.   Kirkhammerton.
Ripley.

Rural Dean, Rev. THOMAS COLLINS, *Vicar of Farnham,*
near *Knaresboro'.*

DEANERY OF RIPON.

Trinity Church, Ripon.   North Stainley.
Aldfield and Studley.   Dallaghgill.
Bishop Thornton.   Hartwith.
Bishop Monckton.   Masham.   When Pecu-
Pateley Bridge.   Kirby Malzeard. liars are abo-
                                          lished, these
Sawley.   Mickley.   will   fall
Markington.   Middlesmoor.   under   the
                                          Rural Dean-
Skelton.   Ramsgill.   ery of Ripon.
Winksley and Grantley.   Grewelthorpe.
Sharow.   Healey.
Dacre.

Rural Dean, Rev. ROBERT POOLE, *Incumbent of Bishop*
Monckton.

D

Clapham Division.

Clapham.	Sedbergh.
Austwick.	Howgill.
Ingleton.	Dent.
Ingleton Fells.	Cowgill.
Bentham.	Bentham Chapel.
Burton in Lonsdale.	Garsdale.
Thornton in Lonsdale.	Cautley.

Rural Dean, Rev. JOHN MARRINER, *Vicar of Clapham, Settle.*

ARCHDEACONRY OF CRAVEN.
Leeds Division.

Leeds, (P. Ch.)	St. Paul.
Armley.	St. James.
Beeston.	Christ Church.
Bramley.	St. Mary, Quarry Hill.
Chapel Allerton.	St. Mark, Woodhouse.
Farnley.	St. George.
Headingley.	St. Luke.
Holbeck.	St. Andrew's.
Hunslet.	St. Philip's.
Wortley.	Little London, (N. D.)
Kirkstall.	Holbeck Subdivision,
Stanningley.	(N. D.)
St. John's.	St. Saviour's.
Holy Trinity.	

Rural Dean, Rev. W. F. HOOK, D.D., *Vicar of Leeds.*

Otley Division.

Otley,	Baildon.
Hampsthwaite.	Bramhope.

Burley.	Horsforth.
Pool.	Fewston.
Leathley.	Thurcross.
Weston.	Thornthwaite.
Guiseley.	Denton.
Yeadon.	Farnley.
Rawdon.	

Rural Dean, Rev. A. FAWKES, *Rector of Leathley.*

Wetherby Division.

Wetherby.	Thorner.
Spofforth.	Shadwell.
Kirby Overblow.	Cowthorpe.
Stainburn.	Kirkdeighton.
Pannall.	Adel.
Low Harrogate.	Barwick in Elmet.
Harewood.	Whitkirk.
Collingham.	Seacroft.
Bardsey.	Roundhay.

Rural Dean, Rev. A. MARTINEAU, *Vicar of Whitkirk.*

Silkstone Division.

Penistone.	Stainborough.
Denby.	West Bretton.
Silkstone.	Cumberworth.
St. Mary's, Barnsley.	High Hoyland.
St. George's, do.	Scissett.
St. John's, do.	Elmley.
Thurgoland.	Darton.
Dodworth.	Gawber.
Cawthorne.	

Rural Dean, Rev. S. SUNDERLAND, *Vicar of Penistone.*

Bradford Division.

Bradford, St. Peter's.	Thornton, Thornton Chapel.
Christ Church.	Denholme Gate Church.
St. John's.	Wilsden.
St. James.	Shipley.
Horton Chapel.	Haworth.
Manningham, St. Paul's.	Oxenhope.
St. Jude's.	Eccleshill.
Bowling, St. John's.	Calverley.
Brierly Chapel.	Pudsey Church.
St. Paul's (But-	St. Paul.
tershaw).	Farsley, St. John.
Trinity (Wibsey).	Idle.
Clayton.	Wyke.

Rural Dean, Rev. JOHN BURNET, *Vicar of Bradford.*

Huddersfield Division.

St. Peter's, (P. Ch.)	Holmebridge.
Holy Trinity.	Farnley Tyas.
St. Paul's.	Linthwaite.
Golcar.	Lockwood.
Christchurch, Woodhouse.	Marsden.
Paddock.	Meltham.
Lindley.	Meltham Mills.
Longwood.	Netherthong.
Scammonden.	South Crossland.
Slaithwaite.	Upperthong, (N. D.)
Almondbury.	Kirkburton.
Holmfirth.	Kirkheaton.
Honley.	New Mill.

Thurstonland. Milnes Bridge.

Armitage Bridge, (N. Ch.)

*Rural Dean,*Rev.JOSIAH BATEMAN, *Vicar of Huddersfield.*

Dewsbury Division.

Dewsbury, (P. Ch.)	Drighlington.
Dewsbury Moor.	Birkenshaw.
Batley Carr.	Heckmondwike.
Hartishead.	Liversedge.
Ossett.	Tong.
Earls Heaton.	Robertown.
Hanging Heaton.	Gomersal, (N. D.)
West Ardsley.	Ossett Green, (N. D.)
Batley.	Mirfield.
Morley.	Hopton.
Gildersome.	Thornhill.
Birstall.	Flockton.
Whitechapel.	Whitley.
Cleckheaton.	

Rural Dean, Rev. THOS. ALLBUT, *Vicar of Dewsbury.*

Wakefield Division.

Wakefield.		Rothwell.	
St. John's.		Middleton.	Parish of Roth-
Holy Trinity.		Oulton.	well.
St. Andrew's.	Parish of	Lofthouse.	
St. Mary, (N. D.)	Wake-	Methley.	
Alverthorpe.	field.	Swillington.	
Thornes.		Garforth.	
Horbury.		Kippax.	
Stanley.		Sandall Magna.	Parish of San-
East Ardsley.		Chapelthorpe.	dall.
Battyeford.			

Rural Dean, Rev. JOHN BELL, *Vicar of Rothwell.*

DEANERY OF CRAVEN.—*Northern Division.*

Arncliffe.	Gargrave.
Halton Gill.	Cold Coniston.
Hubberholme.	Linton.
Kettlewell.	Hebden.
Burnsall.	Kirby Malhamdale.
Coniston.	Skyrholme.
Rilstone.	

Rural Dean, REV. WM. BOYD, *Vicar of Arncliffe, Skipton.*

Southern Division.

Keighley, (P. Ch.)	Kildwick.
St. John's.	Silsden.
Oakworth.	Cowling.
Eastwood.	Ilkley.
Bingley, (P. Ch.)	Addingham.
Morton. } New Districts.	Bolton Abbey.
Cullingworth. }	

Rural Dean, REV. WM. BUSFEILD, *Rector of Keighley.*

Western Division.

Barnoldswick.	Christchurch.
Gill.	Marton.
Bolton by Bolland.	Mitton.
Gisburn.	Hurst Green.
Tosside.	Waddington.
Bracewell.	Grindleton.
Broughton.	Thornton.
Carlton.	Kelbrook.
Lothersdale.	Giggleswick.
Skipton.	Settle.

Rathmel.   Long Preston.

Stainforth   Horton in Ribblesdale.

Rural Dean, Rev. A. DAWSON, Incumbent of Tossett, (*Bolton by Bolland, Gisburn, Blackburn*).

Halifax Division.

Containing the churches in Halifax parish.

This Rural Deanery in abeyance so long as the Archdeacon is Vicar.

NOTE IV.

THE following replies to addresses presented to the Bishop, on two occasions, connected with St. Saviour's Church, convey the sentiments referred to in the text of the Charge:—

THE REPLY OF THE BISHOP OF RIPON TO AN ADDRESS FROM MANY OF THE CLERGY PRESENT AT THE CONSECRATION OF ST. SAVIOUR'S CHURCH, LEEDS, PRESENTED THROUGH DR. PUSEY.

Palace, Ripon, December 26, 1845.

My Reverend and dear Brethren,

I have received, with feelings of grateful satisfaction, the token of your kindness and good will, in the address presented to me from many among the Clergy belonging as well to my own as to other dioceses who were present at the recent consecration of St. Saviour's Church, Leeds; and I have felt the more deeply this expression of your respect and sympathy at the present moment, as it is assuredly one of peculiar difficulty and very anxious trial to all those who bear rule in the Church of this land.

The immediate cause of anxiety for us all, to which you specially allude, is the lamented departure of several of our brethren who have lately forsaken our communion.

It is, indeed, matter for much sadness and sorrow that any of its members should have been so deceived as to lend their talents, (given them, as I truly believe, for far other ends,) to support the cause of ecclesiastical usurpation, of creature worship, and of religious imposture. But, unhappily, their minds being thus overclouded, their affections alienated from the Church, in whose bosom they were born anew to spiritual life, and nourished by the ample means of grace therein mercifully afforded to the children of God, and their influence once exerted to seduce others from their allegiance to her; it is, indeed, well that they have gone out from among us, and can no longer mis-use the power committed to them by our Church to her own hurt and hindrance. For these fallen brethren we shall never, I trust, cease to pray, in the spirit of compassionate love, that their hearts may be led by the Eternal Spirit of Truth to discern the error of their ways, and to return to the fold which they have forsaken.

But their unhappy trespass will, surely, read a lesson of seasonable warning to each of us, and remind us that we cannot with impunity pour contempt upon the Church of our baptism, in which we have grown in grace and in the saving knowledge of our Lord and Saviour Jesus Christ ; that if we wantonly despise the spiritual privileges we have enjoyed within it, instead of thankfully and reverently using them where God has appointed us our place, we may well expect that He will in His anger take them from us ; and that if we will indulge a morbid yearning after an earthly and visible centre of union, while we have the Lord Jesus Christ as our spiritual Head, ever living to dispense to us from above the rich blessings of His covenant of grace, we may be provoking the Lord of Hosts to punish us, as He did the Israelites of old, by giving us over to our own hearts' lusts, and letting us follow our own imaginations. The lamented fall of our brethren will likewise teach us the danger of tampering with practices which may seem to us innocent and even edifying; but of which history and experience have so forcibly proved to us the peril; and which the Church of England has either expressly reprobated or tacitly discountenanced.

For my own part, I confess that I feel little temptation to despondency or discouragement when I look to the many signal marks of God's providential care vouchsafed to our Church, to the truth and purity of the doctrines she teaches, and to the many evidences of spiritual life within her; among which I would thankfully acknowledge the assurance given me by such a body as yourselves, of your anxiety to devote yourselves more earnestly than ever to the duties of your sacred calling in the Church, whose vows are upon you. Let us only hold fast her doctrines of primitive authority, let us but carry out in the spirit of fidelity her recognized teaching, as embodied in that definite expression of Gospel truth set forth in her Liturgy, Articles, and Homilies, remembering that in subordination to the enlightenment of the Spirit of God, we have accepted these as our interpreters of His Holy Word, and we may humbly believe that we shall be safe ourselves, and likewise, through grace, save them who hear us.

I thank you affectionately for the promise of your prayers, which I feel to be especially needed in times when principles, hitherto held most sacred and incontrovertible, are tried and sifted to their very foundation; and I would entreat you to believe, that in all which I have said in reply to your address of kindness and respect, it has been my anxious wish to speak the truth in love. My own imperfect prayers shall in return be willingly offered for you, my Reverend Brethren, that in this season of our trial, you may find your faith confirmed, your hope invigorated; your attachment increasing towards the Church of which you are the ordained ministers, and your hands strengthened in carrying on the heavenly work of winning souls to Christ, among those several flocks over which you are set in the Lord.

I remain,

Your affectionate Brother and Servant,

C. T. RIPON.

THE REPLY OF THE BISHOP OF RIPON TO AN ADDRESS FROM THIRTEEN OF THE CLERGY OF LEEDS, UPON THE SECESSION OF CERTAIN PARTIES RESIDENT IN THE PARSONAGE OF ST. SAVIOUR'S, TO THE CHURCH OF ROME.

Palace, Ripon, Feb. 2, 1847.

My Reverend and Dear Brethren,

I am desirous of acknowledging, with feelings of much gratitude, the expression of your sympathy with me, under the trying circumstances in which I have been recently placed, by the public profession of Romanism in Leeds, on the part of certain persons connected with St. Saviour's Church; and I embrace the opportunity of assuring you how conscious I am that your absence from the consecration of that church was never intended as any mark of discourtesy to myself; while I accept, with the most cordial satisfaction, your declaration of the respect and affection which you bear toward me, as well as of the confidence you repose in my determination to uphold the distinctive principles of our Church as settled at the Reformation.

With regard to the events which have elicited these welcome expressions of kindness and good will, although there is undoubtedly much to grieve, it is nevertheless satisfactory to remember, that no clergyman of the diocese has ever quitted the Church of his fathers to embrace the Romish communion. The ordained person who took this rash step entered the diocese but a short time since, having been sent to Leeds by the leading trustee of St. Saviour's Church, to act there as officiating minister on trial, not only without any licence from me, but even without my knowledge or consent. His services were speedily dispensed with when I discovered his presence there, and ascertained the tone of his mind and the tenor of his proceedings. Yet, short as was his stay, he seems so successfully to have tampered with the faith and allegiance of some few members of the congregation, that they were on the very point of joining him in his act of desertion; and since his departure he has assiduously persevered in his attempts to complete his unfinished work, but happily without effect. Such proceedings, however, cannot but excite feelings of just indignation against the authors of them: while the ignorance thus displayed of the real character and disposition of mind of the individual sent, when consequences so serious were hazarded, must necessarily awaken feelings of distrust as regards any future appointment from the same quarter.

On reviewing the whole case as it presents itself, I cannot but hope that much good may be the issue. The course recently pursued at St. Saviour's seems to me to have been a very dangerous experiment upon the Church of England; and I am willing to believe that its most signal failure will prove a beacon of warning to many who may have embarked in a similar course, convincing them that there is no safety for the belief or principles of any congregation, if a system be introduced which contravenes the spirit of the Church of England, favouring the nearest possible approximation to the Romish faith and ritual, through the revival of obsolete usages never recognized by our Church, and thus rendering the transitiou easy to that reprobated communion; a system which endeavours, in many instances, to substitute a mystical and bewildering excitement that overawes and enthrals the minds of the people, for that reasonable service which is the worship of the understanding as well as of the spirit; a system which habitually presents to the mind ,ideas and shadows, of which our Church has rejected the substance; thereby creating a morbid yearning which can be satisfied with nothing less than the repudiated reality.

Surely, recent events cannot fail to teach all who have fostered such a system, that if they will persevere, in spite of repeated warnings, and multiplied instances of the disastrous consequences, in leading the young, the weak, or the wilful to the brink of the precipice, they are responsible if the dizzy eye or the rash footstep shall plunge their followers in the gulf beneath; nor will the same events less emphatically warn our younger brethren in the ministry to withdraw themselves from the guidance of those dangerous teachers who thus bring them to the verge, if not within the very circle, of perilous error; and should they fall, seem to think that the last act by which they renounce the communion of our Church is the only one which is to be censured or lamented.

Happily, the progress of the evil, in the case immediately before us, has been seasonably arrested. The church of St. Saviour's is vacant by the resignation or departure of all who lately officiated there, and every vigilance and precaution will be used to obviate the recurrence of that which has called forth our animadversions.

May those occurrences, my Reverend Brethren, which have occasioned your address, together with others of a similar character elsewhere, prevail with all who call themselves members of our communion, to cling with a cordial and undivided attachment to the numberless blessings which we enjoy in our Reformed Church; to maintain its unadulterated doctrine and its seemly ordinances, as far as may be, in all their integrity—so that we neither exaggerate that to which it has given no prominence, nor suppress aught which it has emphatically ratified; but accept and use that interpretation of Holy Scripture which is taught in our Articles and Liturgy, in its natural and obvious meaning! May we all devoutly acknowledge the wonderful Providence which enlightened the Fathers of our Church with the beams of heavenly truth, and guided them between the extremes of a blind and indiscriminating superstition, on the one hand, and of an irreverent neglect of all decent ceremonial, a profane contempt for holy seasons and holy places, on the other! Let us show by our lives that those external helps, beyond the recognized usages of our Church, after which many long with an undue desire, are not necessary to purify the heart and elevate the affections, are not essential to the fostering of humility, deadness to the world, and a self-denying love to Christ; but that in all which can adorn the doctrine of God our Saviour, the life-giving verities of His pure Gospel, and a living faith in our crucified Redeemer, can furnish us with the most cogent motives to holiness and obedience.

But beyond this, may these events prove a powerful inducement to brotherly union among all who are faith-

62

ful sons of that Reformed Church whereof we are ministers! And, seeing how much division dissipates the force and efficacy of our labours, let us bring our united energies to bear upon that vast and rapidly increasing population which lies before us. As ambassadors of Christ, let us call upon them with one heart and one voice, beseeching them, in Christ's name, that they be reconciled to God; and may we be mercifully permitted to see much fruit from such combined efforts, in the conversion of many sinners, and in the advancing edification of the people of God!

That such may be the issue of all our doings, my Reverend and Dear Brethren, is the fervent wish and continued prayer of

Your faithful and affectionate friend and brother,

C. T. Ripon.

Note V.

NOTICE OF ACTS OF PARLIAMENT AFFECTING THE CHURCH AND CLERGY, PASSED SINCE THE YEAR 1843.

Substitution of new Churches for old ones.

In cases where a new church is or shall be erected in any parish or chapelry, the statute 8th and 9th Vict. cap. 70, authorises the Church Building Commissioners, on receiving a certificate from the Bishop of the Diocese, and the Patron and Incumbent of any such parish or chapelry, to declare that such new church being duly consecrated shall be substituted for the old or existing church, and to transfer the endowments of such old church to the incumbent of the new one; and the Bishop may issue a commission for allotting pews in such new church to persons who prove their claims to pews in the old church. The incumbent of the old church is to be the incumbent of the new one.

Consolidated Chapelries.

For the purpose of enlarging and amending the Act of the 59th Geo. III. cap. 134, touching the formation of consolidated chapelries, it is provided by the statute 8th and 9th Vict. cap. 70, that where a population is collected together at the extremities of and locally situate in parishes or extra-parochial places contiguous to each other and at a distance from the respective churches of such parishes or places, and there shall be a consecrated church in any such parish or place so circumstanced and situated, the Church Building Commissioners may, with the consent of the Bishop of the Diocese, represent to Her Majesty in Council the expediency of uniting any such contiguous parts of such parishes or places into one consolidated chapelry; and thereupon an Order in Council may be issued to form such chapelry, which shall become a perpetual curacy.

Provision is made for the performance of all the offices of the Church in such consolidated chapelry, and for apportionment of fees, fixing pew-rents, &c.

The Commissioners may in certain cases make grants in aid of the erection of a church for such consolidated chapelry.

Right of Nomination to new Churches.

The Act of the 8th and 9th Vict. cap. 70, contains the following provision on this subject:—

Sec. 23. " And be it enacted, That if before or during the building of any new church or previous to its consecration, the Bishop of the Diocese and the Patron and Incumbent of the parish in which such new church has been or is intended to be built shall enter into an agreement in writing, that the right of nomination to such new church shall on its consecration belong to and be exercised by any body corporate, aggregate, or sole, or by any person or persons, such agreement shall be binding on such respective parties, their successors, and assigns, and they shall be compelled to fulfil the same."

Burial Grounds.

Provision is made by the Acts 8th and 9th Vict. cap. 70, and 9th and 10th Vict. cap. 68, for enabling the Church Building Commissioners to declare that any land conveyed to them for the purpose of being used as burial ground shall be deemed to be part of the parish or parishes for the use of which it shall be obtained, although not locally situate within such parish; and one chapel may be used by different parishes for which burial grounds contiguous to each other shall have been provided.

Drainage of Glebe Lands.

The Acts 9th and 10th Vict. cap. 101, and 10th and 11th Vict. cap. 11, will enable Incumbents, who may be desirous of improving their glebe lands by works of drainage, to obtain an advance of public money for that purpose, provided the patron of the living and the Bishop of the Diocese give their written consent to an application being made under the provisions of these statutes.

THE END.

GILBERT & RIVINGTON, Printers, St. John's Square, London.

A CHARGE

THE CLERGY OF THE DIOCESE OF GLASGOW AND GALLOWAY,

AT THE PRIMARY VISITATION, HELD JULY 4, 1849,

IN ST. MARY'S CHURCH, GLASGOW,

BY

RIGHT REV. W. J. TROWER, D.D.

BISHOP OF GLASGOW AND GALLOWAY.

TOGETHER WITH

RESOLUTIONS ADOPTED IN THE DIOCESAN SYNOD, AND AN ADDRESS
OF THE BISHOP IN RECOMMENDING THEM.

MAURICE OGLE & SON, ROYAL EXCHANGE SQUARE.

1849.

SD - #0060 - 070323 - C0 - 229/152/4 - PB - 9780243034079 - Gloss Lamination